Leading Virtual Teams

20 MINUTE MANAGER SERIES

Get up to speed fast on essential business skills. Whether you're looking for a crash course or a brief refresher, you'll find just what you need in HBR's 20-Minute Manager series—foundational reading for ambitious professionals and aspiring executives. Each book is a concise, practical primer, so you'll have time to brush up on a variety of key management topics.

Advice you can quickly read and apply, from the most trusted source in business.

Titles include:

Creating Business Plans

Delegating Work

Difficult Conversations

Finance Basics

Getting Work Done

Giving Effective Feedback

Innovative Teams

Leading Virtual Teams

Other books in this series (continued):

20 MINUTE MANAGER SERIES

Leading Virtual Teams

Hold people accountable
Build trust
Encourage collaboration

HARVARD BUSINESS REVIEW PRESS

Boston, Massachusetts

HBR Press Quantity Sales Discounts

Harvard Business Review Press titles are available at significant quantity discounts when purchased in bulk for client gifts, sales promotions, and premiums. Special editions, including books with corporate logos, customized covers, and letters from the company or CEO printed in the front matter, as well as excerpts of existing books, can also be created in large quantities for special needs.

For details and discount information for both print and ebook formats, contact booksales@harvardbusiness.org, tel. 800-988-0886, or www.hbr.org/bulksales.

The web addresses referenced in this book were live and correct at the time of the book's publication but may be subject to change.

Cataloging-in-Publication data is forthcoming.

ISBN: 9781633695894
eISBN: 9781633691469

Preview

Leading a virtual team presents a special set of challenges whether you have one team member abroad or several people working remotely. How do you ensure accountability when you don't see your people every day? How do you get them to communicate effectively when time zones, language barriers, and a host of complicated technologies conspire against your team? Distance poses difficulties, but you can overcome these problems and turn them into your advantage. Leading an effective virtual team is possible—and this book will give you quick tips and strategies for managing people productively, no matter where your team is scattered.

Leading Virtual Teams walks you through these important basics:

- Ensuring you have the right mix of skills and abilities on your team for remote work

- Assessing and meeting your team's technological needs

- Clarifying the goals, processes, and norms you'll use to communicate and collaborate with your team from afar

- Regulating the myriad messages and media that enable your team members to work together apart

- Keeping your people motivated, engaged, and accountable despite the distance

- Surfacing and resolving conflict when you can't always see how people are working together

Contents

Contents

Contents

Leading Virtual Teams

What Is a
Virtual Team?

What Is a Virtual Team?

How do you get your people to work together when you can't even get them in the
same city? How do you get past technology glitches to have a productive conversation? Can
you help your staff trust teammates they've never laid
eyes on? How do you maintain accountability with
someone in a different time zone who's going to bed
just as you're getting up? How do you replicate the
small things that knit teams together: following the
same sports teams, saying gesundheit when a sneez-
ing fit erupts, sharing a look over a colleague's absent-
minded humming, even holding elevator doors for
each other? These are just a few of the challenges you
face when you manage a team of remote workers.

You're a leader of a virtual team if you coordinate work around a shared goal—with team members who *don't* share a base of operations. You may be a sales director, managing people who perform the same tasks in different locations. Or perhaps you run a project with a team whose day-to-day responsibilities are as unique as their physical posts. Maybe you manage a handful of off-site employees who work with a core group at the home office. Even if you have one team member working remotely, you're managing a virtual team. And while leading any team involves a mix of people management, technical oversight, and project administration, virtual leaders must perform these functions with blunt communication tools and without face-to-face accountability.

Whether you're a veteran team leader or new to the role, coordinating the work of multiple people in multiple places will scramble your instincts and stretch your skills. But successful leaders make the most of these challenges by orchestrating technologies that meet their group's particular needs and establishing strong norms for how all team members will work together in this virtual space.

Why use virtual teams?

The ubiquity of virtual teams tends to blind us to their usefulness. What are the benefits of this arrangement?

Virtual teams maximize limited resources. By hiring for the short term someone who happens to live in another part of the world, you can ramp up and maintain a steady pace of production for your busy season. Virtual teams help you save on the overhead costs of owning and maintaining a physical plant by partnering with a manufacturer. You can assemble the smarts, staff, and supplies you need to fit your budget and schedule.

They cast a wide net for expertise. Virtual teams allow you to look beyond the resources right in front of you and tap into your organization's global capacities. You might find a technician with a rare skill set—for example, a translator fluent in an uncommon language—or consult a niche expert who can't make an in-person meeting. With virtual teams, you can put boots on the ground to host a client event or supervise a product rollout in a distant place where you do business.

They streamline collaboration. Integrating communication technologies allows the team to interact in whatever way makes the most sense for the individual and the task. When you're face to face with colleagues every day, you don't always think about the most appropriate way to work together—you schedule an hour-long meeting to launch a project, because that's what you've always done. But when your team is dispersed, you're forced to consider the best way for doing what you need to accomplish. If brainstorming sessions in conference calls tend to unravel into people talking over one another, you can initiate a discussion thread on chat and everyone gets a chance to weigh in. And if a complex discussion is bogging down over e-mail, you can set up a video call.

What are the key challenges?

Every team leader struggles to manage personalities while keeping technical work on track. But the virtual environment magnifies the most difficult aspects of running a team. So what challenges do you need to overcome in managing a virtual team to reap the benefits?

Team composition. Some people simply don't thrive in a virtual work environment. If you've inherited an existing team, then you may have some ill-adapted members—people who go MIA when they miss a deadline or who never figure out how to politely jump in on a conference call. Even if you've handpicked your direct reports, you may not know whether someone's a good fit until that person is in the thick of an assignment. Talking to everyone ahead of time about *how* they work—not just what they do—will help you pick the right people and engineer the group norms that will help them succeed.

Isolation. Working remotely can alienate team members from your mission and their peers. Without face time, colleagues struggle to develop trust, and everyone (you, too!) is more vulnerable to loneliness and loss of motivation. A good virtual team leader finds opportunities for team-building in every aspect of the work, making people feel included and that they're working together toward a shared goal.

Technology. Picking the right technology is about removing barriers to the work. Your technology choices will govern how your team communicates and how you share, store, and iterate content. So if your tools are unreliable or otherwise difficult to use—or just don't meet the group's needs—you'll waste time, slow down work, demotivate your team, create confusion and redundancy, and generally make all of you look unprofessional. Gathering input from your partners and team members will help you get your team up and running and working smoothly—with fewer interruptions.

Communication. Without the physical cues that enrich in-person interactions, virtual teams need clear communication norms—which are hard to establish across so many technologies (phone, e-mail, video, chat, and the like). Technology fractures our shared behavioral patterns—what works in person doesn't work on the phone, and vice versa. And colleagues can go days or even weeks without speaking to each other. Meanwhile, when there are no impromptu in-person updates, the sheer volume of messages you receive can be overwhelming. In general, face-to-face communication is always best, followed by video and phone, which are better at capturing emotional information than a written format. But no matter which tool you're using, you'll save time and build goodwill by helping your people find the right channels and develop a shared etiquette for using them.

. . .

This book will walk you through solutions to each of these challenges, so that you can manage your remote team more effectively. The following pages offer step-by-step advice for everything from putting together your team and your technology, to coordinating work and building trust through screens, to mastering communication across multiple technology platforms. And you'll find tips for countering some of the most common problems you're likely to face, such as delivering constructive feedback over the phone.

How you use all these ideas depends on the people you're leading and the work they need to do. So let's start with the fundamentals: making sure you've got the right people on your virtual team.

Get the Right People on the Team

Get the Right People on the Team

Working on a virtual team is not for everyone. While some people embrace the flexibility and independence, others will flounder amid the isolation and technological challenges. Through personal circumstances, management directives, or a simple lack of information, many people who are not well suited to remote work end up doing it. You may or may not be able to move these people off your team.

You might have the luxury of building a team from scratch, or you might be constrained by the personnel decisions you've inherited by taking over an existing team. But whatever the circumstances, you'll want to figure out how to exert the most control over who's in your group, within the boundaries you've been given.

What's important on a virtual team?

All teams need a blend of skills and group rapport, but the technical and personal challenges of remote work demand a special set of traits.

Communication. Strong communication skills are a must. Good virtual team members know how to be precise *and* concise in multiple media, and they err on the side of overcommunication. These skills matter most in core team members, while satellite collaborators and people in niche roles have a lower bar to clear.

Collaboration style. Virtual teamwork requires self-discipline and self-motivation, since team members must stay on schedule and ask for help when necessary. Remote work is not ideal for people who need a lot of supervision.

Temperament. Building productive relationships without the benefit of face-to-face contact requires high emotional intelligence. Look for people who will be generous negotiating conflict in a low-information environment and resilient working alone under pressure. If your team is global, place a premium on cultural sensitivity.

Technology. You want people who are open-minded to new technology and competent in the tools you must use. Evaluate what the team members can teach each other as well as what they have to learn—and what they *can* learn.

Size. When it comes to the number of folks on your team, aim low. Research shows that smaller teams are more effective and more motivated and that virtual teams become particularly unwieldy with more than 10 members. As the numbers rise, communications become too complicated and there are diminishing opportunities to build personal relationships on a team that's distributed across the globe.

Tweak an existing team

You've been given the reins to a team that someone else assembled. Maybe your people have been working together for years under different leadership and have already developed processes for bridging the distance between them. Or perhaps they're as new to each other as they are to you. Either way, before you dive into the work, you'll want to spend time thinking about how your team's members work together.

Evaluate the team members' skills and personal qualities. Paying special attention to the ideal attributes identified earlier, debrief the last leader or consult someone else who knows the team well: a senior member, a supervisor, perhaps even a customer. Track down any written documentation of the team's work, such as an after-action review. Interview team members directly (see the sidebar "Team Survey"). Look for patterns: Which elements of the team are working really well? Where are the obvious pain points?

Identify gaps, and make a plan to fill them. Since you can't directly observe people in action, use the team survey and any other available documentation to make your best assessment. Does anyone require outside training? Can one team member coach another? Do any team roles need to be redefined or reassigned? If the issue isn't too sensitive or if you have good relationships with the rest of the team, run parts of your plan past the team members in one-on-one meetings or by e-mail.

TEAM SURVEY

Choose the questions that are most relevant to your work, and distribute them via e-mail or an online survey tool such as SurveyMonkey, with a due date. Ask for brief, bullet-point answers.

General

- What is your role on this team?

- What skills are most important to your role? Which skills are critical to your success as a virtual collaborator?

- How is your role affected by working remotely? What are the benefits and challenges?

- What do you wish you were better at doing? Which of your talents need to be developed further?

- What are the overall strengths and weaknesses of the team right now, especially with respect to virtual collaboration?

- In an ideal world, how would you adjust your role to add value to the team? Which virtual aspects of your role would you change?

- Ideally, to make your job easier or better, how would you change the way the team works? Which virtual aspects of your collaboration would you change?

Communication

- Which communication tools do you use, and how do you use them?

- Which tools do you feel most comfortable with? What's not working out?

(continued)

TEAM SURVEY

- How easy do you find it to communicate your personal style to your colleagues with the tools available to you? How easy do you find it to get a sense of the personal style of your colleagues?

- What does it look like when an interaction goes well for you? Have you noticed any patterns when interactions go badly?

- How are you coping with time zone differences, language or cultural barriers, or different technology platforms?

Collaboration style

- Which tasks or parts of virtual collaboration are you best at?

- What do you most like to do on the team? What do you most dislike doing?

- What's working for you about how this team works together? What's still hard?

- Overall, would you say you like working remotely?

Temperament

- With whom on the team do you work most closely? How would you describe those relationships, and how has the social distance of remote work affected them?

- Do you have a sense of the temperaments of your colleagues? How did that develop, and what do you think you could do to develop that knowledge further?

- In general, what sorts of people bring out the best in you? The worst? What qualities

(continued)

are most important for you in a virtual collaborator?

- Think about a conflict you've had on this team. How did you handle it? How did the virtual nature of the team play into the way things unfolded?

Technology

- Which internet provider do you use, and what results do you get from an internet speed test?

- What technology do you use to do your work? How would you rate your comfort level with each item or tool you listed?

- Which tools aren't working for you right now? Why?

If you want more detailed input from the team, use the templates in the sidebars "Solicit Group Feedback" and "Ratings Exercise," both near the end of the book, to conduct a holistic preevaluation.

Clearly communicate your plans to the individuals involved and, when relevant, to the whole team. If this discussion happens on a phone call or video chat, document an explanation of the change, and make it available somewhere that's accessible to everyone on the team as a reference going forward.

Confirm your team. Whether you reassign, cut, or add personnel, make sure everyone on the team has roles that are clearly defined and mutually understood. Share a document with a final description of everyone's roles, and if the document incorporates significant changes, schedule a meeting to review it. Encourage people to clarify any uncertainty over their roles by bringing questions to you and any other relevant team members.

Assemble a new team

Sometimes, you're tapped to develop a product, improve a process, or solve a problem. And you're able to cherry-pick folks to do the work. Let's look at how to assemble the right virtual team.

Determine the skills and personal qualities you need. Consult colleagues, supervisors, and direct reports with experience on virtual teams like yours to draw up a list. Use a modified version of the team survey to guide a phone conversation, or send it out via e-mail or an online poll.

Identify people with those skills and qualities. Use your network to look both within and outside your organization. Although team members will be working remotely, location may still matter—for example, your team may need to be in the same time zone or meet certain requirements for internet access.

Recruit your virtual team. You'll approach most people directly, but consider going through a shared contact such as a supervisor or colleague if you're adding someone in your organization: "I'd like to bring Alex on board for this project—since I know you just finished that redesign project together, could you introduce us?" For people you haven't worked with before, make this initial contact as personable as possible—a phone call instead of an e-mail.

Your people are the team's most important re-source by far. But whether they succeed in their mission will depend in large part on the technologies you give them to do their work.

Manage the Technology

Manage the Technology

Technology makes it possible for your team to communicate, coordinate, and build successful working relationships. If you're not a technologist, it's tempting to give this work short shrift: "I'm in advertising, not IT!" But on a virtual team, you *are* IT. In fact, you're the department head. If you work for a small company, no one else is going to solve your connectivity problems or set up your file-sharing software—and you have to be prepared to help your team members do these things, too. If you're part of a larger organization with more technology resources, you'll still play an important role as your people's chief advocate, lobbying IT for support and projects. Establishing the right environment at the beginning of a project will make these tasks easier later on. But it takes time, money, and resources up front.

Assess needs and resources

Your first step is to figure out what your team needs, what resources are presently available to you, and the security policies and restrictions of your company. Evaluating existing resources involves looking not only at what your team members have in place on their end, but also at the tools your organization brings to the table.

Technology touches every element of work on a virtual team, so work through these questions methodically and thoroughly. The sidebar "Assess Your Team's Technology Needs and Resources" structures this process. For each technology domain (such as creating content), list the technologies you *need* and the resources you *have*. Run through the bulleted questions to make sure you haven't skipped over any critical factors.

At the end of this exercise, you'll have detailed notes for each domain. As you make your final selections, keep three principles in mind. First, be cautious about adopting new technology. Using familiar technology will generally save time, keep costs low, and shorten the start-up time for the rest of the team—although some options, especially cloud-based solutions, may save time and money even if they're new to the team. Second, ensure compatibility where it matters. For example, team members working on a written report need compatible word-processing software but don't necessarily have to use the same e-mail service. And third, don't be afraid to make the conservative choice. Simplicity, reliability, and accessibility are often more important than complex functionality.

ASSESS YOUR TEAM'S TECHNOLOGY NEEDS AND RESOURCES

Communicating

- What will be your primary means of communication?

- How will you conduct meetings? By phone? Video?

- What level of internet access will your team members need for communication?

- What capacities will you need on a team site (for example, a wiki page or documentation for ramping up a new hire)?

- Will the team members need to share the same e-mail domain (such as @globalcorp.com)?

- What hardware (such as headsets or web-cams) will the team members need for communication?

- What capacities do the team members need to have on their phones? Do your people need to be on the same mobile operating system (Android versus iOS)?

- Will the team members be required to have a landline?

- How secure will the various channels need to be?

Creating Content

- Which file types will you use?

- What software compatibility will you require?

- Will you need scanning technology?

- Will you need access to any databases?

(continued)

ASSESS YOUR TEAM'S TECHNOLOGY NEEDS AND RESOURCES

- What quality of internet access will your team members need for content creation?

- Which security features will the team need?

Sharing and Storing Content

- How much storage capacity will you need? (The back-of-the-envelope math for storage is as follows: Take the typical file size, multiply it by the number of documents you'll need to hang on to, and the result is your storage requirements.) Should the capacity be scalable?

- Will you store content on hard drives, company servers, or in the cloud (such as Dropbox or Google Drive)?

- Will you synchronize content—updating files automatically across the whole team?

- Will you need versioned documents, that is, the ability to track who made changes?

- Will you need read-only files? Will you need different access levels and permissions for files?

- Will you need compression programs?

- What quality of internet access will your team members need for content sharing and storage?

- What are your group's security concerns, risks, and rules?

Scheduling

- Will you need to share or synchronize calendars?

- Will you need project-management or issue-tracking software (such as Asana, Smartsheet,

(continued)

ASSESS YOUR TEAM'S TECHNOLOGY NEEDS AND RESOURCES

SharePoint, JIRA, Microsoft Project, or Basecamp)?

- What quality of internet access will your team members need for scheduling?

Costs

- What is your budget for all your technology— for its purchase, installation, storage, and maintenance?

- How will you distribute that money across the different technology domains?

- What capital expenses do you have to plan for, versus operational expenses?

- What costs will the organization bear, and what will individual team members pay for?

Seek input

Ultimately, you want technology that capitalizes on what your team already knows how to use. The best way to do this is to talk to your team members directly about their personal needs and resources. You'll get useful technical insights and demonstrate respect and concern for their experiences. So as you assess your team's technology needs and resources, seek feedback from your team members or other key players who will be involved in your work. The team survey will give you some initial information to get started with, but follow up individually with your people to get a better picture. Use their answers from the technology section of the survey, and listen for enthusiasm, confidence, fear, or skepticism: Which of the tools you're considering have they used before? What were their experiences? How open are they to learning something new? How long might it take to get them up to speed? What are they more or less flexible about?

Technology facilitates work not only within a team, but also outside it. Make a list of individuals and organizations your team will interact with and the technology requirements for each relationship. Reaching out to partners is a smart choice for a few reasons:

- You'll find out what technology your partners are already using, so you can pick a compatible tool. "What tool/service/platform do you use for this?"

- You want their advice about a specific selection. "Have you used tools A, B, or C in the past? What was your experience? Do you have a recommendation?"

- You want to inform your partners about a selection you've made that's relevant to them. "We've decided to go with X for file sharing. What's your capacity for this tool right now? Do you need any resources or support from us to set things up? Do you need any training?"

Set up a team site

Whatever other technologies you choose, your team needs a shared digital workspace. It can take many forms—a full-blown website, a file storage service (such as a folder on Google Drive or Dropbox), a messaging and archival system (such as Slack or Hip-Chat), a version-tracking system (such as GitHub), or a combination of tools—but it must cover a few basic functions. Team members need to be able to upload and download shared files as identifiable, individual users on the system (not a shared account with an unsafe password); post key team documents, schedules, and updates; share contact information; and participate in some sort of online discussion threads.

The shared digital workspace isn't just a repository for text that no one wants to read—it should be a vital space where important work gets done. Enforce this boundary by redirecting technical digressions during meetings to the site and by relocating task-related conversations from e-mail and chat whenever possible. When you need input from the team, post your request to the discussion board. If you use it, other people will have to follow suit. And the more integral the site becomes to your collaboration, the more everyone will use it without prodding.

Establish rules for technology use

Once you've selected your team's technologies, lay out a clear set of norms about how they'll be used. Doing so will keep people accountable and help new members assimilate quickly. As you develop protocols for managing content, keep these topics in mind:

- *Naming and organizing files.* How will you make content easily navigable?

- *File types.* Do you need file-type conventions? When should files be read-only?

- *Version control.* How will you ensure that team members are working without redundancy or inefficiency?

- *Access rights.* Who on the team will have access to the various tools, platforms, services, and databases you'll be using?

- *Sensitive material.* How will you safely share and store sensitive or proprietary material?

- *Synchronization.* What materials or tools need to be synchronized?

- *User support.* Who will manage end user issues, and how will the team members escalate an issue?

When it comes to communication technologies, there's even more to think about. Good communication across multiple platforms requires discipline and a common etiquette. Is it acceptable to call colleagues without an appointment to ask on-the-fly questions, or should you e-mail them first? When will team members be available? Who's responsible for setting up conference calls? Whatever you decide, keep these and the following issues in mind as you create protocols for communicating with the team:

- *Venue.* What kind of conversation belongs in an e-mail, as compared with a phone call, a text message, or an online one-on-one or group chat?

- *Audience.* How will you decide which team members need to participate in a phone call or be copied on an e-mail?

- *Availability.* How responsive will you be by e-mail, by phone, or by other channels?

- *Language.* What shorthand will you use to help each other prioritize communications? For example, your group could preface every e-mail subject heading with the name of the project in brackets, so recipients know at a glance what the message is about and can easily organize messages.

- *Coordination.* Who will schedule group meetings such as conference calls or video chats? Who is responsible for maintaining shared calendars?

- *Politeness.* What are the norms of courteous communication, in writing or in real time? For example, is it OK to use BCC in a team e-mail? Are side conversations or interruptions ever acceptable on the phone or on a video chat? What are the rules about emoji?

- *Documentation.* How will you capture meeting minutes and action items? Google Docs? Audio recording? JIRA tickets? Wiki team page?

You don't need to itemize rules for each of these topics—pick the ones that matter the most to you and your team. Be specific about the behaviors you care about, and don't burden the team with rules that are vague or low-impact. (Everyone knows not to send all-cap e-mails.) Write up the protocols in a communications charter that you post to the team site, but let everyone know it's just a first draft: With the help of the whole team, you'll be able to iterate and refine this living document to make it even more useful to your work.

What to do when technology fails

Technology failures are inevitable and can have serious consequences. The trick is to never find yourself caught unawares.

Prepare, test, and practice. Conduct a premortem to catalog major risk points and to play out the worst-case scenario; ask your team members to do one also. Do this at the start of a project or before big meetings or presentations. Brainstorm your contingency plans—your plan Bs—for each pain point: What's your backup video chat service? Your file storage alternative? Do a trial run to make sure these plans are viable.

For basic internet connectivity problems, ask your team to figure out what it can try in the moment. Do all team members know to reboot their computers when all else fails, and do they know how to recover lost files? Ask each person to have a *crisis card* close at hand with information such as their account number with their internet service provider and the contact information for a local, in-home IT service (and find out from your company whether your people need to vet these services ahead of time).

Communicate. Collate and distribute a document with teamwide plan Bs, help links, contact information, and other resources. Make the document generally accessible, and instruct the team to keep the protocol printed out and handy offline. This is one area of virtual work in which a physical artifact is indispensable.

Becoming a self-taught IT department probably isn't why you got into your line of work. But once this work is done, it's time to start in on the part that you really care about.

Get to Work

Get to Work

N ow that you've found the people and resources your team needs, put them to
work. In this chapter, you'll learn how to
bring your team together around a mission and de-
vise rules and routines to keep people collaborating
effectively—even when you're not there.

Launch the team

Every team needs a launch meeting, whether it's a
brand-new group or you're just the brand-new leader.
Get everyone together physically, just this once, if

you can swing it. Face-to-face communication is still better than virtual when it comes to beginning relationships and developing trust. Eye contact and body language help kindle a sense of affinity and trust that will allow a group of strangers to work together before long-term bonds form. You'll also have the chance to assess team dynamics and start setting some behavioral guidelines.

If you can't arrange an in-person meeting, hold a virtual launch. Schedule a generous amount of time, and invite the team to introduce themselves (see the section "Build Rapport and Trust" later in this chapter). Even if you're the only new person on the team, a launch is an opportunity for team members to re-establish their own bonds of friendship and perhaps learn something about each other.

Depending on the available time and the size of the team, consider assigning members to breakout chats to discuss specific aspects of the project or the culture and processes of the team itself. Then bring everyone back into a group chat to report on their discussions. This arrangement puts some structure on a meeting that can all too easily spiral into pointlessness, and it counteracts a natural tendency for everyone to assume the position of an audience member on group chats.

Create a shared vision

Group and breakout conversations during a launch meeting are also a great opportunity to work on the team's sense of purpose. The development of the team's purpose shouldn't be a didactic presentation, but rather a collaborative conversation. So you'll want to work with your team members to describe the purpose of your team in clear, compelling language. Even if your team is working toward a deliverable that has been well defined from the outside, it still has the opportunity to name its mission (Why are we doing this project?) and outline the particulars of the work (What are the details that will make it a success?). These answers matter for every team, but they're especially important to remote workers, who must stave off isolation and stay motivated.

Build your shared vision with a conversation around a few key questions:

- What issue will this project address?

- What's the desired outcome? What benefits will we realize?

- How will the virtual nature of our team allow us to accomplish these goals?

- What are this project's high-level deliverables?

- What lies outside the scope of this project?

- What resources—financial, human, or otherwise—are at our disposal? How will we use these resources to support remote workers?

- What goals and constraints govern the project schedule? What virtual effects do we need to plan for (time zones, team member travel, and so forth)?

- What are the project's key milestones?

- What major threats and opportunities must the project team plan for?

- What special issues does the geographic dispersion of the team present?

These conversations work best in person or on video chat, but you can use the same format in a discussion thread on your team site. Document or bookmark the discussion, and post to the team site a statement of the group's final consensus. As the work progresses and distance chips away at the team's cohesion, revisiting this document will bring everyone back to common ground.

Define common expectations

What does it look like to be a good team member in your group? How much can a team member do on their own before "taking the initiative" becomes "taking over the project"? How long can someone delay answering an e-mail before it starts to impede progress on the work? Is it ever acceptable to swear on a conference call?

Coordinating roles and responsibilities, not to mention plain old-fashioned etiquette, is challenging when your team isn't colocated. The geographical and social distance provides much room for misunderstandings and mistrust to grow—which means, in turn, that your team is extra reliant on the details of task design and work processes to keep things running smoothly.

Start by simplifying the work as much as possible, ideally so that tasks are assigned to subgroups of two or three team members. For each task, clarify the work processes you'll use to accomplish it: Who exactly does what, and when? If your work is cyclical or proceeds in clear phases, periodically conduct an after-action review both to evaluate how things are going and to identify process adjustments and training needs.

You'll also set some ground rules for professional behavior. With a team working in branch offices, basements, and hotel lobbies, people may harbor wildly different ideas about what's expected of them. Table 1 outlines some of the major topics you'll want to cover (for tips about involving your team in this process, see the sidebar "What Input Should Your Team Have on Virtual Norms?").

Align priorities

Your team fits into each member's life in a different way. For ad hoc projects, you're probably adding more

TABLE 1

Setting ground rules

Issue	Question
General terms	• What kind of latitude and independence can team members expect?
	• What resources will be available to them to complete their work?
	• How much will team members be expected to travel?
Hours	• How many hours each day or week will team members work?
	• What times of day are members expected to be available?
	• If your team includes people in different time zones, how will you schedule meetings to accommodate each member?
	• What should members do if they find their responsibilities require them to work overtime or outside their scheduled hours?
Authority and delegation	• Who will be responsible for making what types of decisions?
	• Who has the authority to assign work to specific team members?
Etiquette	• What are the team members' assumptions about appropriate content and language?

Issue	Question
	• What kind of confidentiality or privacy can team members expect from each other, especially since informal communication takes place in the written word more often than on colocated teams?
	• What steps should team members take to redirect e-mails or phone calls when they're away from the office or when their regular hours change?
The unexpected	• How will you plan for periods when you'll have to deviate from these rules? For example, how will you handle a crunch period when the team will need to work overtime?

work to a full plate. With freelancers, you're competing for time with any number of other clients. Even stable teams with full-time members must balance different professional goals and personal commitments. Remote work makes all these dynamics more obscure, so before a project starts, meet one-on-one with your team members to learn about their current priorities and to discuss how these priorities align with the team's shared vision and goals.

WHAT INPUT SHOULD YOUR TEAM HAVE ON VIRTUAL NORMS?

All workplaces need rules, but remote work requires a lot of them. So, who gets to set them? Long distance makes democratic processes more complicated, so be thoughtful about starting an open discussion on norms. A good rule of thumb is to ask for input only when you're genuinely open to using it. That means issues governed by outside constraints, such as budget, are off the table. Soliciting input is time-consuming, so ask questions whose answers are likely to be either brief or extremely important to the success of the project. These dos and don'ts will help you facilitate a productive conversation either way.

Dos

- Have an agenda. Make it clear at the beginning precisely what you're seeking input on.

- Set expectations about how you'll use their responses.

- Present limited choices ("Should we do A or B?").

- Create a document, such as meeting notes or a brainstorming list, that serves as a reference (for you) and a deliverable (for them).

- Follow up with an outcome—even if it's not a popular one.

Don'ts

- Don't ask open-ended questions ("What should we do?").

- Don't initiate conversations you aren't pre- pared to moderate, in person or online. For example, your discussion board will quickly succumb to distraction or petty bickering if no one is minding the store.

TABLE 2

Suggested scripts for talking about priorities with your team

Topic	Question
Professional goals	• "What are you looking to get out of this experience?"
	• "How do you think your work could support our team and organizational goals?"
	• "What professional goals are you working toward right now? How do you see this project fitting in?"
	• "In an ideal world, how would this work further your own professional growth?"
Availability	• "What else is on your plate right now?"
	• "Do you have any deadlines or planned time out of the office coming up that will affect your availability?"
	• "In an ideal world, how would the schedule for this project look for you?"
Personal commitments	• "Do you need any personal accommodations to do your best work?"
	• "In an ideal world, how would this work further your own personal development?"

The kind of questions you ask will depend on your relationship with that person. For example, you can ask someone you directly supervise to show you how they allocate their time each week, but with a freelancer, you can't be so inquisitive. Table 2 suggests questions you might ask your team members to elicit the details you need.

Ambition is a deeply personal thing, and you can't persuade someone to adopt a new career goal to suit your team's needs. Likewise, the boundaries your direct reports have set between their personal and professional lives may be nonnegotiable. For example, if someone gets chronic headaches when working overtime, they may always prioritize their health over your team's schedule. So what can you do to align priorities?

- Can you redefine the team member's role to better fit any professional goals or personal commitments?

- Can you redistribute tasks to better match the person's availability?

- Can you pair the member with collaborators who will balance out any weaknesses?

- Can you rearrange the schedule to avoid panic periods or to take advantage of any synergies across work streams?

- If the person is assigned to multiple teams, can you work with their other supervisors to harmonize your directives?

The earlier you start these conversations, the more flexibility you'll have to tie your people's success and well-being to the work you share.

Build rapport and trust

On traditional teams, the sense of connectedness develops naturally in the interstices of office life—over lunch, in the elevator, during break time, or in pre-meeting chats. But virtual teams lack these casual encounters, so you must make a concerted effort to build rapport and trust.

Fostering team spirit doesn't have to be a big production: Clarify norms, adopt a small set of routines, and stick to them. Use the following checklist as a menu of options, and be realistic in your selections. It's better to do one or two things reliably than start half a dozen you can't keep up with.

❑ *Hold video tours.* Ask new hires to show each other around their workspaces. This practice allows colleagues to form mental images of one another when they're communicating later by e-mail, phone, or text message.

❑ *Share highlights and lowlights.* At the beginning or end of a meeting, ask each team member to talk about one highlight and one lowlight from their workweek.

❑ *Institute personal or professional check-ins.* Invite your team members to give a quick update about themselves at the beginning of each team meeting. Gently enforce the norm that these updates should be brief, but don't discourage personal remarks. If, for example, someone is struggling with an illness in the family, that's good for the team to know.

❑ *Gather for Friday afternoon congrats calls.* This is not very productive for many people anyway, so use it to celebrate the week's accomplishments. Bonus if everyone coordinates consuming a snack or drink during this time.

❑ *Establish "water cooler" chats.* Schedule regular five-minute check-ins a couple times a week, just to catch up. Set up a forum devoted to this sort of casual chat on your team site or any other shared communication channel.

❏ *Ban multitasking.* Set a clear expectation that everyone should be mentally present and engaged during meetings, and follow up by frequently calling on people to share their thoughts. If you're conducting meetings over the phone or by group chat, try switching to video chats. If you know that someone is multi-tasking—you're getting e-mails from them during a conference call—gently and humorously call them out.

❏ *Curb mute-button usage.* Background noise brings humanity into an otherwise sterile conversation—let the barking dog or crying baby be a moment of shared humor or sympathy for your team.

❏ *Appoint someone the team's truth teller.* Add a bit of levity to meetings by turning to the Yoda of the day at critical points during the meeting and ask, "So, what's going on here that nobody's talking about?"

❑ *Reward naysayers.* Pushing back against consensus is hard to do over video or on the phone, so give warm, generous praise to team members who aren't afraid to speak their minds. When everyone appears to be in agreement on an issue, listen for whoever is *not* talking, and solicit this member as a devil's advocate.

Keep people engaged

Your virtual water-cooler chats created beautiful and trusting relationships across the team. But how can you mobilize those social bonds to keep people engaged in, and motivated about, the work at hand?

Foster shared leadership. Assign special projects that team members can share during a meeting, or invite them to run a virtual team-building exercise, such as the weekly highlight-lowlight routine described earlier. As part of your plan to get the right people on the team, ask members to coach one another in their areas of expertise (refer back to your completed team surveys).

Recognize and praise collaborative behavior when you see it. If several people worked together to solve a problem, send an e-mail to the entire team expressing your appreciation and explaining how the work has helped the team overall.

Encourage people to acknowledge each other's work. Praise people for calling out each other's successes. Let them know that recognizing collaboration in others makes them look good, too. Develop norms for how members communicate that they "see" each other's work, and give feedback wherever possible. Even a bland "Thanks," "Nice," or "I'm using this right now" goes a long way. Sharing genuine praise and appreciation is a prerequisite to offering comments that might be more critical: Research suggests the right balance is 10 to 1. Foster candor by supplying team members with the language for criticism, such as "I might suggest . . . " or "Think about this."

Play games. Games provide a low-stakes, fun environment in which team members practice pooling knowledge and coordinating for a common goal. This approach also helps members learn how other members think and act in an accelerated time frame and helps people iterate strategies for working together. For long-standing teams with a gamer culture, consider online role-playing games (RPGs) such as *World of Warcraft*, where team members talk as they play. If RPGs don't fit your team culture, look at mobile multiplayer games such as online *Scrabble*. Even sharing music or book recommendations gives people a chance to explore each other's thinking and connect on a personal level. Team-building activities can feel cheesy—it's the nature of the beast—so encourage people to have a sense of humor about them: "It's East Coast versus West Coast in *Scrabble* this week!"

Build a team with rhythm. Work in a physical office has a natural tempo: You see colleagues in predictable places at predictable times, you do certain kinds of work at the same time every day, you attend meetings with familiar people in familiar rooms. When some or all the members of a team are working remotely, it's all too easy to feel disconnected without these patterns. One antidote is to be disciplined in creating and enforcing routines in virtual team work. Hold regular meetings, ideally on the same day and at the same time each week, starting and finishing on time. Make the meeting agendas routine where possible, and share them ahead of time. Good meeting practice matters more when you have a dispersed team, because following the rules helps create those shared expectations and experiences. Establish regular check-ins by e-mail or group message: an end-of-week e-mail update, or a two p.m. "How's it going?" text.

These practices depend on having a nimble and well-adapted communications strategy. Next, we'll explore the major challenges in this realm.

Communicate
Effectively

Communicate Effectively

C ommunicating with your team involves a trade-off between two mandates. On the one hand, you're compensating for the information loss that happens when a team doesn't work in the same physical space. On the other hand, you need to limit the amount of time the team spends on the apparatus of virtual work—sending and receiving e-mails, participating in video chats, and so on.

The general rule is to overcommunicate when you're working remotely: Document everything, share freely, keep everyone informed. But what does this practice look like at the decision-making level? Where's the line between sharing the right amount of context and asking your team to scroll through lengthy missives? This chapter outlines strategies for walking that line and for troubleshooting when you find yourself offside.

Pick the right channel

With a large (and proliferating) range of communication options at your disposal, you have to live by the rules you've set for how your team communicates. As team leader, you have an outsized influence on your group's dynamic: You send more messages to more people, about more topics, than does anyone else on the team. If you have any bad habits, they will be felt and possibly adopted by more people.

Being articulate goes a long way, of course, but on a virtual team, good communication depends largely on the format you choose. To some extent, this is common sense: Most people know not to leave detailed, nuanced instructions in a voicemail or to send a colleague a text with game-changing bad news. But many circumstances are not as clear-cut, and when you send dozens of e-mails a day, it's easy to lose sight of the impact each message has on your people's workflow.

Ultimately, you want your team to develop an instinct about which communications tool is appropriate in a given situation. That means thinking through the purpose of a message and its likely effect on the recipient. Everyone on the team can use the five questions in table 3 to build good habits.

Work around time zones and linguistic and cultural barriers

The global reach of a virtual team is one of its best features, but it can wreak havoc on communications when there's no recognizable workday. To keep things

TABLE 3

Find the right channel for your message

Question	Answer	Channel
How important is my message?	I need or want to document the exchange.	E-mail, text, instant message (IM), or team site
	It's pretty disposable.	Phone call, voicemail, or video chat
How complicated is my message?	I can say it in a sentence or two.	E-mail, voicemail, text, or IM
	It's fairly detailed, and it will probably require explanation and clarification with my team.	Phone call, video chat, shared document (such as a Google doc), or e-mail with attachment
How urgent is my message?	I need an immediate response.	E-mail with a flag or a clear subject line ("URGENT: quick call this afternoon?"), phone call, voicemail, text, or IM—whichever you think the person will be most responsive to
	It can wait; I don't want to disrupt the team's work.	E-mail, a scheduled phone call or video chat, or team site
What input do I need?	Some, maybe from several team members.	Phone call or video chat; team site, if input doesn't need to be simultaneous
	None; this is a one-way message.	E-mail, voicemail, text, IM, or team site
What emotional impact will my message have?	None; it's pretty banal.	E-mail, voicemail, text, IM, or team site
	I expect a strong reaction, positive or negative.	Phone call or video chat

moving across multiple time zones, schedule face time with team members who aren't in your time zone, even if it means making video calls at times that are inconvenient for you. For teams with some overlap, agree on a window of time when everyone—no matter what their location is—will be at work and reachable.

For teams with no overlap, orchestrate an information handoff. What does each group need to know about the previous shift? Consider sending short teamwide e-mails in a standard format, in addition to person-to-person connections between key players.

Remote work also magnifies linguistic and cultural barriers. With relatively few contextual clues (no body language or facial expressions), misunderstandings can be even more common. And because so much communication is opt-in—choosing to log into chat, for example, compared with running into someone in the hallway—it's easy to sweep those misunderstandings under the rug. Your people may be reluctant to expose themselves on conference calls or video chats with awkward questions or to push back against someone they don't know well. It's so easy to just keep quiet.

The most effective solution to these problems, of course, is to build trust within your team. While you work on that, you can help everyone perform their best by paying attention to how they choose to communicate.

Talk individually to your team members about their preferences. What formats are they most comfortable using? What do they expect in terms of accessibility and responsiveness?

Tailor communication formats to each person's language abilities. Find what works best for your people, and use it. For example, don't conduct detailed conversations over e-mail or group chat if someone prefers speech to reading and writing.

Build on existing relationships or affinities. You don't need to create perfect harmony across the whole team. Instead, encourage team members to find allies who can help them navigate what's unfamiliar and to develop new networks.

Avoid communication fatigue

Remote work generates a lot of traffic, and staying on top of it can be exhausting and divert attention from priority projects. Help your team find the right balance by promoting communication that builds motivation. Live communication such as phone and video calls takes a high level of mental and emotional engagement, and with so many other, low-touch options available, phone or video is often the last resort. But e-mail and the like can't match the emotional connection and intellectual engagement that real-time interaction supplies. So convenience and efficiency shouldn't always trump more personal methods of communication. Encourage collaborators to schedule regular meetings with each other to provide this vital experience.

At the same time, reduce communication that saps motivation. Some conversations are necessary but boring—ask anyone who has sat on a co-op board. By its nature, remote work makes these experiences worse. Because information can't circulate informally as it does in an office, it's pushed out in wave after wave of agendas, updates, and reports. If you don't like participating in these conversations live, you'll loathe having to follow them through endless e-mail chains and discussion board threads.

Limit the amount of energy you're asking your team to put toward these demotivating conversations. Designate specific times and places as "receptacles" for this kind of exchange, and keep them out of normal communication channels as much as you're able. Try the following strategies as well.

Segment conversations about process. These discussions can become quite freewheeling, but breaking them up across different communication platforms can save time and heartache for everyone. Start by soliciting input on a discussion board or a shared document: What's working? What are the pain points? What changes would people like to see? Then draw up a draft process, and share it with the team before your next group meeting. Gather feedback over the phone or a video chat, and iterate the whole sequence as needed.

Routinize updates. Move your team toward brief status reports or bulletins—give them a template. Post these to a dedicated spot on the team site.

Institute virtual office hours. Make yourself available to the whole team for a few hours each week, when people can talk to you about whatever is on their mind. Keep the time consistent, if you can, and let everyone know how to get in touch with you (text and group chat are a good choice, since they're instantaneous but not intrusive). Show people how to use this time by redirecting off-topic or random remarks to it: "Good question, Peter. I'd like to save it for office hours this week. OK, back to the agenda . . ."

Clarify emotions. It's easy to misinterpret a message when you can't read facial expressions or body language, and whether you're angry, hurt, or just confused, you're wasting energy and time. Regardless of context, turning emotional subtext into plain text will help the team avoid the kind of passive-aggressive exchanges everyone loathes: "Paul, you seem adamant about this point. Are you frustrated with how the issue was handled last time around?"

Find the right balance

You may get feedback that your communication style isn't working for everyone on your team. Maybe your people feel smothered (they can shrug off overanxious calls from a colleague, but not from you), or maybe they're desperate to get more than terse texts about tomorrow's big meeting. Either way, your habits are harming their productivity.

If you find you're *overcommunicating*, ask yourself these questions:

- *Are you compensating for a perceived skill gap somewhere?* If so, evaluate whether that perception is apt, and make a plan to fill the gap.

- *Do you not trust the rest of the team to communicate with each other?* Back off for a couple days to see how things function without your extra effort. Where you see problems, solve them by helping team members build the skills and habits they need to make it work independently.

If you find you're *undercommunicating*, ask yourself the following questions:

- *Does everyone on the team see the big picture?* They may need less contextual information from you on a day-to-day basis if they share a common vision and understand, at a high level, how the team is going to execute that vision.

- *Are you overscheduled?* Delegating will open up more time in your schedule to do the necessary work of sending e-mails, fielding calls, and so on.

Mastering how to communicate with a virtual team takes time, and of course, things won't always go smoothly. In the next chapter, you'll learn practical tips for coping with some of the common problems that you'll face.

Cope with Common Problems

Cope with Common Problems

Missed deadlines. Sloppy work. Infighting. These problems plague all teams, but when you supervise remote workers, too often you don't know that something is wrong until it's really wrong. So much of what's happening—such as poor time management and passive-aggressive e-mails between colleagues—is invisible to you. And because your view into how your people work is so limited, your team members may feel more pressure to appear in control. They might hide problems because they don't want you to see how the sausage gets made or because they think something is their fault when it's truly a larger issue affecting the whole team, such as a software malfunction.

To push past the virtual veil, you'll need to develop proactive habits and an eye for trouble. In this chapter, you'll learn best practices for evaluating performance, maintaining accountability, and managing conflict in ways that help you counsel team members when they falter, and get your whole team to thrive.

Evaluate performance from a distance

In traditional offices, there's a bias to base performance assessments on the presence of the employee around the office. Do they come in early and leave late? When you walk by their desk, do they look busy? Obviously these cues aren't available on a virtual team. Instead of watching *how* people work, you're seeing *what* they produce—the number of sales they've made, the code they've written, the video they've produced. But this information can be misleading, too. Sure, the video looks great, but did your team member collaborate well with the sound engineers? Did they appropriately credit others' contributions? Good work can't come at the cost of unprofessional or even illicit actions.

The main challenge for you, then, is to find ways of observing behavior you can't actually see. What strategies will work best?

Take notes. Because team meetings carry so much weight in a virtual environment, it's difficult to pay attention to performance unless something remarkable happens. But because these are the most information-rich interactions you'll have with your team, you need to capture what happens. When you take meeting notes, write down each team member's name on a notepad to keep track of the comments, questions, and suggestions that stand out to you. (If it's too distracting to take detailed notes during a meeting, write down your observations immediately afterward, when they're still fresh in your mind.) If someone is stubbornly making the same point over and over again, make a note. If someone brings up a problem no one else has thought of, make a note. If someone gives a coworker credit for doing good work, make a note. You're creating a detailed performance record and raising your own awareness around group dynamics.

If you're using other communications technologies that create a written record, treat the team's interactions there the same way you would a meeting. Check in on group chats or discussion boards periodically to see who's giving useful feedback or mediating conflict—and write it down. Because you *will* forget, and without a written record, bias can easily overpower experience.

Limit self-evaluations. Without regular feedback from others, your team members have only their own perceptions of their work to go on. We all tend to overrate our abilities and take credit for good results while denying the bad—tendencies that you, as a leader, can't correct for when so much of the work process is invisible to you. So even if the home office includes written self-evaluations as part of its performance assessment process, evaluate whether they're right for your team's situation, and dial them back accordingly.

Get group feedback. Team members know a lot about each other's work—information that you don't know, especially in an environment with no opportunity for you to casually observe collaborations. If your team members know and trust each other, solicit their feedback as a group exercise over a phone or video chat, and invite colleagues to speak directly to one another (see the sidebar "Solicit Group Feedback"). If the team isn't close enough to pull that off, ask for their input through e-mail, a closed chat, or an anonymous poll. In either scenario, be clear with the whole team about the process, and administer it across the board.

SOLICIT GROUP FEEDBACK

Ask your team members to respond to these questions with respect to one another's overall performance:

- How did this person contribute?

- What do you want this person to stop doing?

- What do you want them to start doing?

- What do you want them to continue doing?

- What are their strengths as a virtual collaborator? Their weaknesses?

That way individuals won't feel blindsided or picked on by the group.

The questions should be fairly open-ended. For more detailed answers around a standard set of metrics, ask the team to rate one another (see the sidebar "Ratings Exercise"). Administer it privately by e-mail, a closed folder on the team site, or a private poll.

RATINGS EXERCISE

Instruct your team members to evaluate one another using the following criteria on a scale of 1 to 10 (weakest to best). Ask them to explain their thinking for each response and to share any suggestions about how the colleague could improve or how the team could be better organized to mitigate performance problems.

This team member . . .

_____ Adhered to team rules, including those about how we collaborate virtually

_____ Fully contributed to our shared vision and team culture, making their presence felt, no matter where they were

_____ Completed tasks on time and with care

_____ Was self-motivated and able to keep things moving even when we weren't in the same place

(continued)

RATINGS EXERCISE

_____ Engaged in and supported team decisions

_____ Used collaborative technologies appropriately and with skill

_____ Communicated well across a variety
of platforms

_____ Gave and received feedback appropriately
in multiple media

_____ Negotiated conflicts and promoted harmony, online and in person

_____ Made an effort to build productive relationships with colleagues despite the
distance

Maintain accountability from afar

Like all work, virtual collaboration includes its share of missed deadlines, poor results, and interpersonal conflict. What's different for virtual team leaders is the impersonal context in which these performance issues take place. To hold people to their commitments when other assignments or bad habits get in the way, you'll use the same strategies you would if you worked in the same location: documenting shared expectations, agreeing on accountability processes, giving regular feedback, and following up on an explicit improvement plan if it becomes necessary. But managing a troubled team member is an intimate process, requiring copious time, attention, and empathy—all resources that are best spent face to face, where physical proximity strengthens the relationship. So you'll need to compensate for the lack of these cues at each step.

Follow up on anomalies. If someone is struggling or behind, there are probably some other behavioral cues: They're uncharacteristically quiet on a team call, they increase or decrease the frequency with which they communicate, or they seem especially anxious, frustrated, or checked-out. You may also become aware of what they're *not* doing: Are they strangely relaxed before a major deadline? Are they booking light hours in crunch time, when everyone else is slammed? When something seems off, don't wait. Pick up the phone.

Check in. Light-touch communication tools such as texting and instant messaging (IM) carry lower emotional stakes than a face-to-face conversation does, so use them to follow up more assiduously than might feel acceptable in person. If you call someone into your office to ask them how they're doing with challenging new software, they might feel put on the spot. But a brief text ("How'd it go using the new system?") lets you touch base without intimidating them.

Beware, however. For this technique to work, you need to be relentlessly positive in your framing. A harried employee will read "Are you on track for Friday's deadline?" as aggressive and maybe even mistrustful, but "Looking forward to seeing the product demo on Friday! Anything you need from me?" communicates enthusiasm and a team mind-set.

Talk to other members of the team—tactfully. Colleagues will have a different vantage point on what's happening, but approach them circumspectly. In addition to any specific questions you have about the problem at hand, try to get some general context by asking open-ended questions.

- "How is the project with Akhil going overall?"

- "How are you finding him as a collaborator?"

- "Akhil has been doing a great job generally, but recently I've wondered if there's more I can do to support his engagement. Have you observed anything that might help me? I'll keep whatever you say confidential."

- "You mentioned that Akhil has been less engaged in the work recently. When did that issue start? What do you think is going on there?"

This kind of conversation works best by phone or video chat, not the least because coworkers may not want to leave a written record of their complaints and speculations.

Meet with your team members to talk about the problem. Just as you do with team members who work with you in the same office, you must address performance issues with remote workers with sensitivity. Broaching the topic might have unexpected emotional fallout, so set up a meeting in person—if possible—or over video or phone. Getting face to face will give you more information about what the team member is thinking and feeling and allows you to project the emotions you want the person to perceive—empathy, trust, concern, firmness, and so on.

Prepare as you would for any other feedback conversation: Focus on behaviors, practice your language ahead of time, probe for root causes, and close the conversation by agreeing on an improvement plan. Document what happened in a follow-up e-mail or private chat.

Manage conflict on a virtual team

Like teams in any other workplace, virtual teams experience conflict, but arguments play out differently when people don't have face-to-face relationships. That can be good, because it limits the opportunity to engage in office politics. But because online communication disinhibits antisocial behavior, task-related disagreements—simple arguments about how to do something—are more likely to devolve into interpersonal conflict. And while conflicts about tasks are usually easy to resolve and may ultimately be good for the work, interpersonal conflicts are tenacious and toxic. Following are some ways to surface and solve task conflicts before they sour work relationships.

Maintain an online discussion board. Create a place to hold active discussions about disagreements, so that team members have the chance to address important issues as they arise. These conversations simulate what happens casually when everyone is physically in the same office. Boards can also take advantage of online disinhibition, since people are more willing to voice pushback behind the safety of a screen. Think of it as preventative medicine: Transparency builds trust when issues are discussed openly and resolved according to their technical merits.

Mediate interpersonal conflicts in person, if possible. Sometimes, individuals can't work it out on their own, and then the fix is simple but hard: mediation, either by you, another supervisor, or someone with conflict-resolution experience. Again, in-person mediation is ideal, or you can try video or phone if the parties can't meet in the same place. In face-to-face meetings, arrange the seating at evenly spaced intervals to avoid an us-versus-them physical setup. And if you can't meet face to face, establish clear rules of engagement. Without eye contact, participants are likely to interrupt each other. Moreover, a slow internet connection can exacerbate the problem. So set expectations that you'll actively moderate the call and will make sure that each person gets equal time by calling on folks directly, or by sending a detailed agenda that shows how each party will get equal airtime.

Practice active listening. Active listening is a set of techniques that promote full, honest, and transparent discussions, and in the low-information interactions of virtual work, it's especially useful. The general principle is to iteratively check your understanding by reflecting back what you see and hear. This is especially useful in drawing people out if you're not face to face. Here are some examples:

"You seem worried about . . ."

"If I understand, your idea is . . . Did I get the essence of it? If not, please tell me more."

"It sounds like your main concern is . . ."

"These seem to be your main points: . . . Is that right?"

Use these phrases in written communications, too. It's also helpful to summarize phone and video discussions on an electronic whiteboard, live chat, or shared document. Periodically restating basic ideas gives other people a chance to clarify misunderstandings. And acknowledging the emotions that are driving a disagreement allows people to express concerns they might otherwise withhold.

Separate people who just can't get along. Not all conflicts are solvable. If people with intractable problems must collaborate, insulate their work from each other as much as possible, and find a communications option that works best for them. If the presence of other team members lessens the tension, encourage them to communicate via the team website or during weekly conference calls. If they struggle with real-time conversation, ask them to e-mail instead of trying to text or IM.

. . .

Success with leading a virtual team, like so much of leadership, is a matter of experimentation. With new skills and a nimble mind-set, you'll continue to push your abilities in every direction, learning from your remote partners and the individuals on your team. You can't prepare for every snafu that leading a virtual team will present, but with the right tools and the right people by your side, you'll reap the benefits of a close team—no matter how physically remote the members may be.

Learn More

Quick hits

Dixon, Nancy. "Combining Virtual and Face-to-Face Work." HBR.org, July 1, 2015. https://hbr.org/2015/07/combining -virtual-and-face-to-face-work.

Even if you mostly work with your team remotely, chances are that you *can* convene in person—at important milestones, for example, or to conduct a field trip. Dixon, whose research helped pioneer the field of knowledge management, shows you how to get the most out of each type of interaction by "oscillating" strategically between virtual and in-person meetings.

Ferrazzi, Keith. "How to Build Trust on Your Virtual Team." HBR.org Video, July 14, 2015. https://hbr.org/video/236359 3491001/how-to-build-trust-on-your-virtual-team.

Virtual collaboration disrupts the team-building patterns you're used to seeing in a traditional office: You can't organize a team lunch, for example, or seat two key collaborators next to each other at a meeting and watch them hit it off. Ferrazzi, a strategic consultant who focuses on professional relationship development, zeroes in on this challenge and outlines four research-based tips for fostering trust between people in far-away places.

Samuel, Alexandra. "Things to Buy, Download, or Do When Working Remotely." HBR.org, February 4, 2015. https://hbr.org/2015/02/things-to-buy-download-or-do-when-working-remotely.

If you or your team members are working outside the office—at home, at an alternate worksite, or on the road—you'll want social media expert Alexandra Samuel's practical tech tips for staying connected and focused away from your base. Remember all the little things that can make or break your day on the go, from putting that extra charger in your car to setting up an emergency communication channel for SOS messages from your team members.

Books

Harvard Business School Publishing. *Giving Effective Feedback* (20-Minute Manager Series). Boston: Harvard Business Review Press, 2014.

Talking about performance issues is one of the hardest parts of any team leader's job, and the social distance that technology introduces into these conversations doesn't help. This book walks you through the basics of giving good feedback no matter what the environment is. You'll learn how to pick your moment, engage your employee in a two-way dialogue, respond to negative reactions, and follow up on next steps.

Samuel, Alexandra. *Work Smarter, Rule Your Email*. Boston: Harvard Business Review Press, 2014.

You and your team probably spend more time each day using e-mail than any other tool. Samuel details how to get the most out of this experience. She shows how you can reengineer your settings to see important e-mails first and to make attacking the backlog of unread and unanswered mail a manageable task. Once your team members have cleaned up their inboxes, they can stay on top of incoming messages by developing habits for incorporating e-mail–related tasks into the rest of their workdays.

Saunders, Elizabeth Grace. *How to Invest Your Time Like Money*. Boston: Harvard Business Review Press, 2015.

Managing the communications apparatus of a virtual team can become a bottomless time sink. If you or one of your team members struggles with this, Saunders can help. Learn to impose discipline on communication and other work activities, so that you consistently put your greatest effort on where it can do the most good. Use the proven techniques and principles of personal finance to figure out how you're wasting time now, what a more productive schedule would look like, and how to improve your time management.

Articles

Ferrazzi, Keith. "Getting Virtual Teams Right." *Harvard Business Review*, December 2014 (product #R1412J).

This comprehensive article combines research-based insight (Ferrazzi surveyed over 1,700 knowledge workers for this piece) with a deep understanding of the human relationships that underlie all teamwork. Ferrazzi highlights communication and transparency as key themes for the virtual leader, and you'll learn how to maximize these quantities at every point in your team's life cycle, from staging a kickoff to welcoming a new member onboard.

Johns, Tammy and Linda Gratton. "The Third Wave of Virtual Work." *Harvard Business Review*, January 2013 (product #R1301D).

It's a good idea to pull back for a broader view of the economic and organizational trends that created the virtual team you're leading today. Johns and Gratton look at how virtual work has evolved, and they outline how companies should arrange their space, talent, and workflows to make the most of these changes. While this article takes a higher-level perspective on virtual work, you'll gain concrete insight into the dynamics governing your colleagues' day-to-day experiences.

Majchrzak, Ann, Arvind Malhotra, Jeffrey Stamps, and Jessica Lipnack. "Can Absence Make a Team Grow Stronger?" *Harvard Business Review*, May 2004 (product #R0405J).

Most advice on leading virtual teams focuses on how you can replicate the dynamics that make face-to-face collaborations so successful. But sometimes difference is good. Majchrzak and her coauthors show that by pushing tools that allow your people to hold ongoing, threaded discussions, you can bypass inefficient meetings and foster creativity and initiative in trusted colleagues. Your team becomes even more productive apart than it could ever be if all the members were in the same place.

Sources

Primary sources for this book

Ferrazzi, Keith. "Getting Virtual Teams Right." HBR.org, January 22, 2015. https://hbr.org/webinar/2015/02/getting-virtual-teams-right.

Harvard Business School Publishing. Harvard Manage-Mentor. Boston: Harvard Business School Publishing, 2002.

———. *Pocket Mentor: Leading Virtual Teams* (Pocket Mentor Series). Boston: Harvard Business Press, 2010.

Other sources consulted

Berry, Paul. "Communication Tips for Global Virtual Teams." HBR.org, October 30, 2014. https://hbr.org/2014/10/communication-tips-for-global-virtual-teams.

Blake, Robert R., and Jane S. Mouton. "Overcoming Group Warfare." *Harvard Business Review*, November 1984 (Product #84603).

Sources

Ferrazzi, Keith. "Evaluating the Employees You Can't See." HBR.org, December 20, 2012. https://hbr.org/2012/12/evaluating-the-employees-you-c.

———. "How to Manage Conflict in Virtual Teams." HBR.org, November 19, 2012. https://hbr.org/2012/11/how-to-manage-conflict-in-virt.

———. "How Virtual Teams Can Create Human Connections Despite Distance." HBR.org, January 31, 2014. https://hbr.org/2014/01/how-virtual-teams-can-create-human-connections-despite-distance.

Harvard Business School Publishing. *HBR Guide to Coaching Employees (eBook + Tools)*. Boston: Harvard Business Review Press, 2014.

———. *HBR Guide to Project Management (eBook + Tools)*. Boston: Harvard Business Review Press, 2015.

Majchrzak, Ann, Arvind Malhotra, Jeffrey Stamps, and Jessica Lipnack. "Can Absence Make a Team Grow Stronger?" *Harvard Business Review*, May 2004 (product #0405J).

Maruca, Regina Fazio. "How Do You Manage an Off-Site Team?" *Harvard Business Review*, July–August 1998 (product #3685).

Shapiro, Mary. *HBR Guide to Leading Teams*. Boston: Harvard Business Review Press, 2015.

Watkins, Michael. "Making Virtual Teams Work: Ten Basic Principles." HBR.org, June 27, 2013. https://hbr.org/2013/06/making-virtual-teams-work-ten.

Index

Index

Notes

Notes

Notes

Notes

Notes

Notes

Notes

Notes

Notes

Notes

Smarter than
the average guide.

Harvard Business Review Guides

If you enjoyed this book and want more comprehensive guidance on essential professional skills, turn to the **HBR Guides series**. Packed with concise, practical tips from leading experts—and examples that make them easy to apply—these books help you master big work challenges with advice from the most trusted brand in business.

- Better Business Writing
- Coaching Employees
- Finance Basics for Managers
- Getting the Mentoring You Need
- Getting the Right Work Done

- Managing Stress at Work
- Managing Up and Across
- Office Politics
- Persuasive Presentations
- Project Management